LIVING WITH
LEARNING
DISABILITIES

by Amy C. Rea

ReferencePoint
Press®

San Diego, CA

For more information, contact:
ReferencePoint Press, Inc.
PO Box 27779
San Diego, CA 92198
www.ReferencePointPress.com

Content Consultant: David K. Urion, M.D., Associate Professor of Neurology at Harvard
Medical School, Director of Learning Disabilities/Behavioral Neurology Program at Boston
Children's Hospital

LIBRARY OF CONGRESS CATALOGING-IN-PUBLICATION DATA

Name: Rea, Amy C., author.
Title: Living with Learning Disabilities / by Amy C. Rea.
Description: San Diego, CA : ReferencePoint Press, Inc., [2019] | Series:
   Living with Disorders and Disabilities | Audience: Grade 9 to 12. |
   Includes bibliographical references and index.
Identifiers: LCCN 2018011537 (print) | LCCN 2018011837 (ebook) | ISBN
   9781682824825 (ebook) | ISBN 9781682824818 (hardback)
Subjects: LCSH: Learning disabilities—Juvenile literature. | Learning
   disabled children—Juvenile literature.
Classification: LCC RC394.L37 (ebook) | LCC RC394.L37 R43 2019 (print) | DDC
   616.85/889—dc23
LC record available at https://lccn.loc.gov/2018011537

CONTENTS

TWO STORIES OF LEARNING DISABILITIES

Savannah Treviño Casias hated math. Even in kindergarten, she had trouble learning to count. The struggle continued though elementary school. In sixth grade, she was tested to see whether she needed special education services. Savannah hoped she wouldn't. "To me, getting special education would have meant I was dumb, incapable—that there was no hope for me," she says.[1] She thought special education was only for dumb kids.

The tests showed that Savannah had dyscalculia. Dyscalculia is a learning disability that affects someone's ability to work with numbers and mathematical concepts. For Savannah, that meant she had trouble remembering things like that "five" and "5" are the same thing. Identifying patterns, such as organizing things from largest to smallest, was a struggle.

Children with dyscalculia struggle with numbers and mathematical concepts. This includes challenges with identifying patterns and remembering numbers.

The middle school special education program was initially unsuccessful for Savannah. She told herself she didn't need help, but at the same time, her struggles with math hurt her self-esteem. When high school started, Savannah realized she had to change. "I was tired of hating math," she says. "I was tired of thinking I was inadequate."[2] Savannah decided to accept her learning disability. She got help. Special education gave her skills and tools that helped her learn.

As Savannah worked to improve her math skills, her self-esteem also improved. "Every day, I told myself it was okay that I learned at a different pace and in a different way than the other students," she says.[3] Sometimes she had different lessons and homework than her classmates had. But she still studied and learned new concepts.

> "I know I will have to work smarter and harder than others because of my learning disability. But I also know that I will continue to embrace my dyscalculia as an important part of who I am."[4]
>
> *–Savannah Treviño Casias, who has dyscalculia*

By the time she moved on to college, Savannah understood that dyscalculia would always be part of her life. It didn't have to stop her from succeeding. Asking for help didn't make her a failure. "As I sat waiting to meet with my college disability advisor, I felt a sense of pride," she says. "I know I will have to work smarter and harder than others because of my learning disability. But I also know that I will continue to embrace my dyscalculia as an important part of who I am."[4]

Finding Success in School

Adam Ninyo had always struggled with handwriting. "It's often said that doctors have messy handwriting," he says. "By that logic, as a senior in high school, I should have a medical school diploma."[5] Instead, at age seventeen, his handwriting looked like a preschooler learning to write for the first time.

Adam has dysgraphia, a learning disability that makes it difficult for him to write by hand. No one is certain what causes dysgraphia. People with this learning disability have trouble taking information from their brains and putting it on paper. For Adam, that meant difficulty with writing letters in a straight line or staying within margins. He also had trouble keeping words going from left to right on a page, understanding and remembering spelling rules, reproducing shapes, and reading maps.

He and his family worked with special education programs to try to improve his handwriting. But even after years of trying, Adam didn't have the fine motor skills necessary for clean handwriting. So he took a different approach. His school allowed him to use a computer for assignments. When he took tests, the school had someone write down the answers he gave instead of having him write the answers himself.

"We don't live in a world where we must climb every mountain, or handwrite every paper. We live in a world in which innovation triumphs over natural ability," Adam says. "A few years from now, I'll be finished with college and preparing for a job or graduate school."[6] Like many people with learning disabilities, Adam has chosen to focus on using his skills. While he may struggle in some areas, he can plan for the future and succeed.

Savannah and Adam are two real-life examples of how learning disabilities can affect a person's life. Not all students with learning disabilities have the same problems. There are many different kinds of learning disabilities. Some affect how a student processes information, while others make it hard for students to communicate. But learning disabilities do not mean a student is dumb or can't learn. There are many tools and techniques available to help all students learn.

Chapter 1

WHAT IS A LEARNING DISABILITY?

People can be diagnosed with learning disabilities at any age. No matter when the diagnosis takes place, it can lead to many questions. People with learning disabilities and their friends and family benefit from doing research to understand these disabilities and the many ways they affect a person's life.

What a Learning Disability Is Not

Many people have misconceptions or wrong information about learning disabilities. Learning disabilities are not a lack of intelligence. In fact, according to the Learning Disabilities Association of America (LDAA), people with learning disabilities are generally of average or above-average intelligence.

People with learning disabilities often have above-average intelligence. But they can still struggle in school because of their disabilities.

However, that intelligence does not always translate to academic success. The LDAA says, "There often appears to be a gap between the individual's potential and actual achievement."[7] Many types of learning disabilities are not obvious to other people. A student with learning disabilities might struggle with some aspects of schoolwork while excelling in other areas. In those cases, people might assume the student is just being stubborn or lazy.

Learning disabilities are also different than physical disabilities. "Learning disabilities should not be confused with learning problems which are primarily the result of visual, hearing, or motor handicaps," says the LDAA.[8] For example, a child with hearing loss might have trouble following a teacher's instructions. But that problem is not classified as a learning disability.

The organization LD OnLine provides information on learning disabilities. Its website also clarifies some misconceptions regarding learning disabilities. "[Learning disabilities] should not be confused with lack of educational opportunities like frequent changes of schools or attendance problems," the website says.[9] A student who has missed significant amounts of school might be behind other students, but that situation is not classified as a learning disability.

A learning disability is also different than a language disorder, but the two are increasingly thought to be related. A language disorder affects how language is processed in the brain, which can affect both what someone says and what they hear others saying. However, the disorder that causes a child to have difficulty processing language can in turn make it more likely that they'll be diagnosed with a learning disability later. When children have trouble hearing and processing language, their abilities to interpret and work with language can be impaired.

"How can a kid know everything there is to know about dinosaurs at the age of four, but still be unable to learn the alphabet?"[10]

–Corinne Smith and Lisa Strick, authors of Learning Disabilities: A to Z

At first, learning disabilities may seem to have no explanation. "How can a kid know everything there is to know about dinosaurs at the age of four, but still be unable to learn the alphabet?" write Corinne Smith and Lisa Strick in the book *Learning*

Disabilities: A to Z. "How can a student who reads three years beyond her grade level turn in written work that is incomprehensible? How can a child read a paragraph aloud flawlessly and not remember its contents five minutes later?"[10] To understand learning disabilities, people need to look beyond the surface.

Defining Learning Disabilities

A learning disability is a neurological disorder. Neurology is the study of the nervous system, which includes the brain, spinal column, muscles, and nerves. A neurological disorder is caused by something malfunctioning in the brain, causing physical or psychological symptoms.

Many people with learning disabilities are born with a neurological disorder. Occasionally, neurological disorders can develop after birth. Regardless of when they occur in a person's life, someone with learning disabilities has a brain that functions differently than the brain of someone who is not learning disabled. The way her brain receives and organizes information can make things like reading, spelling, and reasoning harder to do.

For example, a person with dyslexia may look at the same text someone else reads, but the dyslexic person's brain interprets the text differently. The nondyslexic person's brain sees "9" as "9," while the dyslexic person's brain might interpret the "9" as a "6." This also happens with letters and words; the nondyslexic person's brain sees the word "no," while the dyslexic person's brain may interpret that word as "on." These changing brain interpretations can have an enormous impact on the dyslexic person's ability to keep up at school. Different types of learning disabilities involve the brain's interpretation of things, making it challenging to approach schoolwork and many parts of daily life.

This is why it should not be assumed that people with learning disabilities are less intelligent than their peers. Michael Brian Murphy, an author with learning disabilities, lists several ways a learning disability can affect a person. Someone with a learning disability may face challenges in "not understanding what the skill is, not understanding how to perform it, not being able to perform it," or other issues.[11]

Imagine that someone is asked to kick a ball. The person might not know what the ball is or how to kick it, or they might be unable to balance while kicking. The process of kicking a ball seems simple, but if someone has trouble with one part of the request, the entire process becomes difficult. People with learning disabilities can have a hard time learning things the way other people do. It may take more trial and error for them to find ways for their brains to process new learning.

Learning disabilities can cause people to struggle with things like reading, writing, math, and social cues. It's easy for others to assume the person isn't smart, doesn't try hard enough, isn't cooperative, or isn't paying attention. But they don't understand that people with learning disabilities may always struggle with certain skills.

It seems like it should be simple for adults to recognize the signs of learning disabilities. But learning disabilities come in all different shapes and sizes. *Learning disabilities* is considered an umbrella term. That means the phrase refers to several conditions, each with its own characteristics and challenges.

Social Effects of Learning Disabilities

Learning disabilities can lead to social or emotional problems. A student with learning disabilities might be teased by classmates. Adults might pressure kids to just work harder without understanding the situation.

"Although many children with learning disabilities are happy and well adjusted, some do develop related emotional problems," Smith and Strick say. "These students become so frustrated trying to do things they cannot do that they give up on learning and start developing strategies to avoid it."[12] Students might feel that they're stupid and can't be helped. Some students might respond with anger, while others might become anxious or depressed.

Untreated learning disabilities increase the risk of social isolation, low self-esteem, and loneliness. Emotional problems can affect students' perception of themselves and their work. In some cases, anger, depression, and loneliness can overshadow the learning disability itself.

The book *Learning Disabilities: A to Z* includes the story of one girl, Casandra, whose learning disability led to emotional problems. She remembers struggling to learn the alphabet at age five. "As I got older, reading and spelling got harder and harder for me. Teachers, my

> "[Some students with learning disabilities] become so frustrated trying to do things they cannot do that they give up on learning and start developing strategies to avoid it."[12]
>
> –Corinne Smith and Lisa Strick, authors of Learning Disabilities: A to Z

family, and friends all seemed to be picking on me all the time," she recalls.[13] Her academic struggles affected her social life: "Since everyone wanted to laugh or blame me for things, I stopped trying to read either to myself or out loud and became a clown in school and stayed to myself at home."[14]

Casandra realized on her own that she was not stupid. She learned to manage her disabilities and graduated from high school. But the emotional effects lingered. Casandra was still scared of reading and speaking to people into her late twenties. The effects of untreated learning disabilities can be difficult to overcome.

Support Systems

There is no cure for learning disabilities. But there is an increasing amount of help and support available. Strategies and techniques to manage these disabilities are available and can help learning-disabled students grow.

In 1975, the US government created policies to protect students with learning disabilities. A new law required all public schools to offer free education to special-needs students in the least-restrictive environment possible. That means children with disabilities must be given the same educational opportunities as children without disabilities. Schools must provide the necessary services to accomplish that. That may involve assistance with academics, speech, or language. It can also include adaptive technology that can help a disabled child overcome obstacles to learning and even transportation to and from school. Modifications can be made in the classroom or to the curriculum as well. That law became known as the Individuals with Disabilities Education Act (IDEA). IDEA includes conditions known as "specific learning disabilities." The law also covers other disabilities, some physical and some social. Experts have varied opinions on what conditions are considered specific learning disabilities. According to the LDAA, there are seven specific learning disabilities: auditory processing disorder, dyscalculia, dysgraphia, dyslexia, language processing disorder, nonverbal learning disabilities, and visual perceptual/visual motor deficit.

IDEA has led to several changes in public education. Today, more than 62 percent of children with disabilities of any kind spend at least 80 percent of the school day in a regular classroom. Many students work with Individualized Education Plans, or IEPs. IEPs are developed for each specific student who will use one. They are personally designed with a number of factors in mind, including the student's learning disabilities and educational goals. An IEP may involve adaptive technology or modifications to curriculum. For example, a student with dyslexia might be allowed to listen to an audiobook for a class rather than having to read the book.

IDEA also has led to programs for infants and preschool children with early signs of disabilities. Early Intervention Programs are designed for children from birth to age three who show early signs of disabilities. This includes children who are considered "developmentally delayed," which can include delayed learning of things like speech, cognitive skills, and motor skills. No young child

People with learning disabilities may have low self-esteem, especially if they don't have resources to help them with their disabilities. These students may feel angry, lonely, anxious, or depressed.

develops at exactly the same rate. Some children demonstrate certain skills sooner than others. A child who is considered developmentally delayed has fallen behind the regular range of skill development. They may also have multiple areas in which they are delayed. In other cases, very young children may use Early Intervention Programs when they have health conditions that can lead to disabilities, including birth defects and genetic disorders. In these cases, an Early Intervention Program can involve physical therapy, occupational therapy, speech therapy, medical visits, hearing or vision services, or home visits, among other things. When a child in an Early Intervention Program turns three years old, he or she becomes eligible for the IEP process.

It's important for people with learning disabilities to have their conditions identified and to receive support. The National Center for

Learning Disabilities (NCLD) reported in 2014 that only 68 percent of students with a learning disability graduate from high school, compared with 83 percent of students overall. Students who drop out of high school and don't graduate face much lower odds of being successfully employed, are likely to earn less money, and are likely to be less healthy and have a shorter life expectancy.

Prevalence of Learning Disabilities

The National Institutes of Health (NIH) and the US Department of Education estimate that roughly 15 to 20 percent of all Americans are affected by learning disabilities. The National Center for Education Statistics reported in 2017 that 14 percent of young people ages three to twenty-one received special education assistance through public schools. *Special education* is a broad term covering learning disabilities, physical disabilities, emotional issues, or social concerns. Analyses of special education enrollments by the Department of Education's Office of Special Education Programs in 2016 show that 34 percent of special education students have been diagnosed with some form of learning disability. It can be hard to determine exactly how many people have learning disabilities because some people may be undiagnosed or misdiagnosed. There are also differences in the ways each US state sets guidelines for diagnosis.

Another obstacle to diagnosis is that some people aren't aware of learning disabilities. Dyslexia, which affects reading ability, has been well-publicized over the years. A 2017 NCLD study found that 80 percent of parents surveyed had heard of dyslexia. The same study found only 13 percent of parents had heard of dysgraphia. Only 11 percent had heard of dyscalculia. The study shows that dyslexia affects 5 to 17 percent of children, while dysgraphia affects 7 to 15 percent. However, since fewer people are aware of dysgraphia, it often goes undiagnosed. Parents may look for signs that their child has trouble reading but not recognize other signs of learning disabilities.

Not only are people uninformed about learning disabilities, they are unaware of tools that are available for support. Only 42 percent of parents in the NCLD study had heard of IEPs, despite the fact that schools are required to provide them for qualifying students. Even if someone is diagnosed with a learning disability, he might not have access to all the resources available.

Learning disabilities can affect all genders and ethnicities, but some groups are diagnosed more than others. The NCLD reported in 2014 that two-thirds of students identified as having learning disabilities were male. African-American and Hispanic students were disproportionally represented. For example, in Nevada, 16 percent of students diagnosed with learning disabilities are African American, but African Americans make up only 9.9 percent of the student body. There also appears to be a higher level of diagnosis among students who identify as multiracial or who do not specify their race. However, many researchers feel learning disabilities should be expected to appear equally across races and ethnic backgrounds. Researchers are trying to determine why some groups are diagnosed more than others.

One possible reason is that people of color are more likely to live below the poverty line. Some studies have shown a link between low incomes and disability diagnoses. When students of color are also in low-income groups, it's possible that they are more likely to be diagnosed as disabled through bias. Testing methods might also be biased against minority groups. For example, a student who is learning English as a second language might be misdiagnosed as having a learning disability because she can't understand the test questions. An additional problem is that students of color are more likely to be in separate special education classes than Caucasians, even though studies have shown that keeping learning-disabled students in the general classroom has a positive effect on their ability to progress.

Learning disabilities are varied and complex. They can be undiagnosed or misdiagnosed, and when that happens, it can lead to people being labeled stupid, lazy, or disorganized. Learning disabilities can be managed through various techniques once they've been identified. That's why it's important to understand how these disabilities manifest in people.

Learning Disabilities in Fiction

Author Rick Riordan has several characters with learning disabilities in his Percy Jackson series. Some of his characters have dyslexia, a condition that makes reading difficult. On his website, Riordan says, "Dyslexic kids are creative, 'outside-the-box' thinkers. They have to be, because they don't see or solve problems the way other kids do. Making Percy dyslexic was my way of honoring the potential of all the kids I've known who have those conditions. It's not a bad thing to be different. Sometimes, it's the mark of being very, very talented."

Quoted in Amanda Morin, "11 Great Quotes About Dyslexia," *Understood.org*, n.d. www.understood.org.

Chapter 2

WHAT CAUSES LEARNING DISABILITIES?

Determining what causes learning disabilities is a difficult science. Dr. David Urion, a researcher at Boston Children's Hospital, says, "There appears to be no one cause of learning disabilities."[15] Researchers do know that multiple factors can combine to play a role in the development of a learning disability. Some causes seem related to genetics, as dyslexia and similar disabilities can be passed down from parents to children. Additionally, babies who are born premature are at a higher risk for learning disabilities. Low birth weight, which is a symptom of premature

> "There appears to be no one cause of learning disabilities."[15]
>
> –Dr. David Urion, a researcher at Boston Children's Hospital

birth, is an indicator of high risk for learning disabilities. Complications during pregnancy, such as illness or injury that can affect the infant, can also increase chances of disabilities. Another risk factor is if the mother uses alcohol or drugs during pregnancy.

Exposure to lead as a child has been linked to learning disabilities. The most common source of lead poisoning is lead-based paint and lead-contaminated dust in older houses. But lead can also be found in some home health remedies, imported products, drinking water, and home repair items involving car batteries. Lead exposure is especially dangerous for young children whose brains and bodies are still developing. That's partly due to the fact that young children absorb four to five times as much lead as adults do from the same lead source. Lead can attack the brain and the central nervous system, causing irreversible damage. This includes damage that can result in learning disabilities.

It's unclear whether there is a direct genetic cause behind learning disabilities. There appears to be a growing body of evidence that shows learning disabilities may run in families. Researchers are still working to determine if that's because there's a genetic link or because children unconsciously pick up behaviors they see from their parents and older siblings. It's also difficult to directly connect learning disabilities within families because there are often differences. For example, a parent with a learning disability that affects their ability to write may have a child who has speech comprehension difficulties. That could indicate that while the predisposition to have a learning disability is genetic, the particular learning disability is not.

Many causes of learning disabilities are unknown, and no risk factor is a guarantee that a person will have a learning disability.

When it's hard or impossible to isolate a specific cause, searching for a cure is difficult. Some things, including most social factors, have been ruled out as causes. "Learning disabilities are not caused by economic disadvantage, environmental factors, or cultural differences," says Sheldon Horowitz of the NCLD.[16] While those factors may affect the diagnosis rate for learning disabilities, they are not causes. Instead, researchers have focused on biological factors that contribute to learning disabilities. Biological factors can be roughly divided into four groups: brain injury, brain development issues, chemical imbalances, and heredity.

"Learning disabilities are not caused by economic disadvantage, environmental factors, or cultural differences."[16]

—Sheldon Horowitz of the National Center for Learning Disabilities

Brain Injury

Brain injury or brain damage can come from a variety of causes, including head trauma, concussions, high fevers, strokes, and brain tumors. Brain injury has been found to cause learning disabilities. Diseases that affect the brain, such as encephalitis or meningitis, have also been found to sometimes lead to learning disabilities. There are a variety of conditions that can affect the brain, ranging from malnutrition to chemotherapy treatment for cancer. Situations in which the brain is deprived of oxygen for too long, such as choking or drowning, can also be related to learning disabilities. In some cases, the learning disability is masked under physical symptoms. For example, a child who had a brain injury could be diagnosed with seizure disorders as a result of the injury. But that same child may not be examined for learning disabilities, even though those can also result from the injury.

Brain injury can occur before birth. When a pregnant woman comes down with a disease like measles or develops gestational diabetes, the disease could potentially harm the infant's brain. Prenatal exposure to drugs, alcohol, and cigarettes is also a risk factor for some conditions.

Brain Development

Issues in brain development are also linked to learning disabilities. Before birth and as a child grows, the different parts of the brain learn to work and communicate with each other. That allows children to begin developing verbal and physical skills as their brains mature. The brain depends on the signals that pass between brain cells to communicate. These neural connections that form as a child grows are critical for processing information. But sometimes these connections do not form, or they may form abnormally, leading to learning disabilities. "Why developmental errors and delays occur is not always clear," write Corinne Smith and Lisa Strick in *Learning Disabilities: A to Z*. "Events that disturb prenatal brain development are undoubtedly responsible for some abnormalities. In other cases, heredity appears to play a role."[17]

Researchers have identified abnormal brain activities that seem to be linked to learning disabilities. These abnormalities can happen in one or more sections of the brain, including the left hemisphere, the right hemisphere, and the frontal lobe. As an infant grows and learns, the different parts of the brain become more specialized. Yet each part connects and communicates with the other parts of the brain. If one area does not develop properly, whether naturally or due to illness or injury, that area's specialization may falter.

For example, the brain's frontal lobe manages things like self-control and focus. In the brain of someone with a condition like attention-deficit hyperactivity disorder (ADHD), the frontal lobe may be smaller, or it may not process information efficiently and effectively. When the neurons in the frontal lobes are underactive, it causes problems with motor skills, attention, impulse control, and planning and organization. "Problems of this kind affect children's readiness for classroom instruction, and they create an overall impression of immaturity even when the children are capable of functioning at a high level intellectually," Smith and Strick say.[18]

> **"Problems of this kind affect children's readiness for classroom instruction, and they create an overall impression of immaturity even when the children are capable of functioning at a high level intellectually."[18]**
>
> —Corinne Smith and Lisa Strick, authors of Learning Disabilities: A to Z

That's in contrast to potential problems with the left temporal and parietal lobes. These work to match sounds to symbols as well as to memorize things like written words. Students with reading-based disabilities may have underactive left temporal and parietal lobes, and those lobes may not communicate well with other parts of the brain.

The cerebellum handles movement and balance, as well as fine motor skills. When this area is not functioning properly, it can cause people to have trouble balancing or doing simple tasks such as writing or tying shoes. The parietal lobes on both the right and left sides work with numbers and math. If these lobes are less active than usual, it can cause difficulty with math-related work.

Chemical Imbalances

A neurotransmitter is a chemical agent released by a neuron, which is a type of cell that receives and sends messages between the brain and other parts of the body. That chemical agent allows information to be spread through the brain and central nervous system. If something interferes with the neurotransmitters, it can cause the brain to not process that information properly.

Researchers are finding evidence that these types of chemical imbalances in the brain are involved in some learning disabilities. Such imbalances particularly affect attention spans, organizing and planning, and hyperactivity. The American Medical Association found that people with ADHD may have low levels of dopamine markers. Dopamine is a chemical that, when released in the brain, provides a feeling of pleasure or reward. People are motivated by that feeling. When dopamine is low, it can cause people to feel unmotivated or unfocused.

Heredity

Heredity may also play a role in learning disabilities. Studies show that about 40 percent of children diagnosed with learning disabilities also had a parent or sibling with similar disabilities. Another study of children with reading disabilities found that 88 percent had a relative with a similar disability. But how heredity works is a complex topic that is still undergoing further research. There are many ways that learning disabilities could be hereditary. Unusual brain anatomy, patterns of brain maturation, and higher susceptibility to illnesses that can affect brain function are all possible hereditary connections.

However, research still hasn't conclusively found an actual genetic link. It's possible that heredity plays some role, but it may go hand-in-hand with environmental influences. There are researchers who feel that heredity is not ever going to be considered the single cause of a learning disability, and that environmental factors go hand-in-hand with heredity.

A student with nonverbal learning disabilities says, "My mother certainly seems to have some 'word nerd' qualities, as well as being anxious and sensory-sensitive to smells, tastes, and is often bothered by labels. My father is somewhat of a narcissist, and quite often is insensitive to other people's feelings, and sometimes doesn't pick up on social cues."[19] More studies are needed to determine the impact of heredity in learning disabilities.

While learning disabilities are largely a function of the brain, they're also affected by environmental influences. Some such influences include the home environment and whether someone receives affection and encouragement within the home, as well as adequate nourishment and medical care. In addition, receiving support and encouragement in the educational environment plays a role for the student. The lack of these things will not cause a learning disability. But for the student with a learning disability, lack of physical and emotional support makes the disability harder to cope with and manage.

Some possible causes of learning disabilities can be identified when children are young. This can include brain development problems or heredity.

Symptoms of Learning Disabilities

There are several signs that someone may have a learning disability. These symptoms vary across age groups, as brain development continues and changes during growth. That's one of the things that makes diagnosing learning disabilities difficult. Another complicating factor is the fact that there is not a straightforward list of specific symptoms that fit every person. Even if there were, many people have multiple disabilities in varying degrees of severity. Then there are students who try to hide the difficulty they're having. They're more likely to complain about homework or insist on not going to school.

Learning-disabled children age ten and younger may speak later than most children and have difficulty with pronunciation. Their vocabulary grows more slowly. They can have trouble learning things like the alphabet, numbers, colors, or shapes. Remembering facts or learning new skills can be more difficult for them. They may also have impulsive behaviors, difficulty with planning, or poor physical coordination.

For children ages eleven to thirteen, symptoms of learning disabilities can include difficulty with handwriting and with written math problems. They may have a strong desire to avoid reading out loud or writing. They may frequently reverse letter sequences. For example, someone with dyslexia may see the word "cat," but their brain interprets it as "tac." Children this age with learning disabilities may also have a hard time understanding body language and facial expressions. Because of this, it can be hard for them to make friends.

High school students and adults exhibit similar symptoms. Spelling continues to be a problem, and they may continue avoiding reading and writing tasks. They frequently have trouble with open-ended questions on tests. Adapting to new settings can be a challenge. They may pay either too little or too much attention to details and misread information. These general symptoms are used to help discover whether a person has a learning disability of some type. Some symptoms are common across several disabilities.

Auditory Processing Disorder

Auditory processing disorder (APD), also known as central auditory processing disorder, affects how the brain interprets sounds. The issue isn't hearing loss. Instead, the issue is with how the brain

Some students with learning disabilities may have trouble socially. They may have difficulties making friends.

manages the information it receives from the ears. A person with APD has trouble distinguishing between different sounds in words or interpreting where those sounds are coming from.

This can lead to a number of related symptoms. A person with APD has difficulty focusing on oral presentations and trouble blocking out background noises. Complex sentences or sentences that are spoken very quickly can be hard to understand. Following a sequence of directions or instructions is also a challenge. The person may tend to process thoughts and ideas slowly and struggle to explain them.

Language Processing Disorder

Language processing disorder (LPD) is a form of APD that only affects language processing. APD has to do with how the brain interprets all sounds coming in from the ears, including things like background noises and music. But LPD only affects the processing of language. People with LPD have trouble understanding meaning from spoken language, as well as difficulty expressing thoughts out loud themselves. LPD also causes problems with reading comprehension and with writing out concepts. People with LPD often can describe or draw an object, but they can't produce the word that names it. Even something like understanding jokes can be difficult.

Dyscalculia

Dyscalculia affects a person's ability to understand mathematical concepts. This includes telling time, counting money, recognizing patterns, and understanding word problems and fractions. Even longer-term time concepts, including seasons and months, can be hard to understand. Carrying numbers over or dividing a number into another number can also be stumbling blocks for a person with dyscalculia. "A lot of people say, 'I'm not good at math' because they couldn't handle pre-calculus or something," says cognitive

> "A lot of people say, 'I'm not good at math' because they couldn't handle pre-calculus or something. People with dyscalculia struggle to tell you whether seven is more than five."[20]
>
> –Edward Hubbard, cognitive neuroscientist at the University of Wisconsin–Madison

neuroscientist Edward Hubbard of the University of Wisconsin–Madison. "People with dyscalculia struggle to tell you whether seven is more than five."[20] Their brains don't process quantitative differences the way most people's brains do.

Dysgraphia

Dysgraphia affects a person's ability to do handwritten tasks and other activities that involve fine motor skills. One of the more obvious symptoms is poor handwriting, both for printing and for cursive writing. But dysgraphia also includes inconsistencies in how someone writes. She may mix upper- and lower-case letters inappropriately, or mix print and cursive. When she writes letters, the letters may vary in size or tilt. There may be unfinished words, or words with missing letters in the middle. Someone with dysgraphia has trouble seeing how letters are formed in their mind before trying them on paper. They also tend to have a lot of trouble with thinking and writing at the same time. Among other things, this makes taking notes during class lectures difficult.

Dyslexia

Dyslexia is one of the best-known learning disabilities. Reading comprehension is affected by dyslexia. The brain of a person with dyslexia struggles to process the order of letters on a page. Sometimes the dyslexic brain will switch letters around in the mind. This makes learning to spell and to read more difficult. It can also affect someone's ability to work on math problems. There's a disparity between the person's ability to understand written language versus understanding the same text when it's read to them. A person with dyslexia has much better comprehension when he doesn't have to read something himself.

Nonverbal Learning Disabilities

Nonverbal learning disabilities (NLD) cause problems with motor skills, visual-spatial skills, and social skills. Someone with NLD may have very strong verbal communication skills, but they may have trouble interpreting nonverbal cues such as body language and facial expressions. She may also interpret things very literally and have difficulty with metaphors and puns. NLD also disrupts a person's ability to follow directions, and she may get lost easily. Someone with NLD can learn to respond appropriately to social cues but still not understand them. "We NLDers can laugh when others laugh, and wince when we see someone get slammed, just like everyone else, but it is the ability, or lack thereof, to understand emotions—not only our own but others'—that's the problem," says Michael Brian Murphy, author of *NLD from the Inside Out*.[21]

Visual Perceptual/Visual Motor Deficit

Visual perceptual/visual motor deficit is often found in people with dysgraphia and NLD. It affects how someone understands what he sees and how he translates what he sees into writing and drawing. People with this condition cannot accurately copy something. Frequently they put their paper at odd angles or turn their heads while working on paper. Writing letters is a struggle that often results in messy, misaligned text, or reversed letters (for example, *d* for *b*). They grasp their writing utensils very tightly and often break pencils or

SPECIFIC LEARNING DISABILITIES

Type of Learning Disability	What Does It Affect?	Symptoms
Auditory Processing Disorder (APD)	how the brain interprets sounds	trouble focusing on oral presentations, trouble blocking out background noise, difficulty understanding someone who speaks quickly, difficulty following directions
Dyscalculia	understanding of mathematical concepts	difficulty telling time, difficulty counting money, trouble understanding patterns, difficulty practicing math problems
Dysgraphia	handwriting abilities and other fine motor skills	poor handwriting, difficulty expressing ideas through writing, difficulty taking notes
Dyslexia	reading comprehension	trouble reading, trouble learning to spell
Language Processing Disorder (LPD)	how the brain processes language	trouble understanding spoken language, difficulty expressing thoughts verbally, problems with reading comprehension and writing
Nonverbal Learning Disabilities (NLD)	motor skills, visual-spatial skills, and social skills	trouble interpreting body language and facial expressions, interpreting conversations very literally, difficulty following directions
Visual Perceptual/ Visual Motor Deficit	how people understand what they see and how they translate what they see into writing or drawing	trouble copying things, messy handwriting, holding writing utensils tightly

According to the Learning Disabilities Association of America, there are seven specific learning disabilities: auditory processing disorder, dyscalculia, dysgraphia, dyslexia, language processing disorder, nonverbal learning disabilities, and visual perceptual/visual motor deficit. These learning disabilities have a wide range of effects on the mind and body, and their symptoms can take many different forms.

crayons while writing or drawing. They often feel their eyes itch or burn while reading, or find that words and letters blur.

Related Disorders

There are several other conditions that affect learning. Attention-deficit hyperactivity disorder (ADHD) is not considered a specific learning disability. However, research has found that roughly 30 to 50 percent of students with ADHD also have a specific learning disability. ADHD causes a person to have difficulty focusing and paying attention. It can also involve hyperactive behavior and an inability to control impulses. When combined with a specific learning disability, ADHD can make learning even more challenging.

A person with dyspraxia has difficulty controlling muscle movements. This affects larger movements like coordination and walking. It also affects smaller movements like language and speech. A person with dyspraxia appears to be clumsy, frequently stumbles, and has poor hand-eye coordination. Dyspraxia also affects fine motor skills. That can make it harder to do things like color within the lines or complete jigsaw puzzles. It can also make someone more sensitive to noise, including sudden loud noises and ongoing background noises. Sensitivity to scratchy, rough fabrics and materials is often a symptom. Dyspraxia is often diagnosed along with dyslexia, dyscalculia, or ADHD. As children with dispraxia mature into adulthood, they may develop increased difficulty with spoken language, including organizing what they're saying. They can also have problems with memory, focus, and the ability to follow instructions, which indicates a shift from motor difficulties to cognitive difficulties.

Some conditions are not technically learning disabilities, but they affect students' learning. Someone with ADHD may have trouble paying attention in class.

Problems with executive functioning are commonly found in people with learning disabilities or ADHD. These kinds of problems include difficulty planning, organizing materials and time, and paying attention and remembering details. Combined with a learning disability, problems with executive functioning can make learning more stressful and difficult.

A student with NLD explains the difficulty of having issues with executive functioning: "It is incredibly difficult for me if they change the bell schedule in school for any reason—like an assembly or a

> "It is incredibly difficult for me if they change the bell schedule in school for any reason—like an assembly or a teachers' meeting or something."[22]
>
> —A student with nonverbal learning disability

teachers' meeting or something. I know where I am supposed to be at any given time on a particular day, but if they switch the schedule from an 'A' day to a 'B' day, I get very, very anxious."[22]

Characteristics

One report by the National Association of Special Education Teachers listed common characteristics of people with learning disabilities, based on several studies. It is important to note that not every person with learning disabilities has all of these characteristics. Having some or most of these characteristics does not mean someone can't be successful in a classroom.

Academic achievement deficits generally fall into one or more of three categories: reading, math, and written expression. Language deficits can affect oral expression and listening comprehension. Either of these situations can affect a person's ability to communicate successfully with others.

Achievement discrepancy refers to people with learning disabilities who are known to have comparable intelligence to their peers. But with this discrepancy, they struggle to maintain the same kinds of academic achievements as their peers. There are several potential reasons for this. Memory issues can be a problem. So can cognitive deficits that involve difficulty organizing and planning. Other learning-disabled students may have metacognition deficits.

Metacognition involves the skills needed to identify strategies to complete a task, implement those strategies, and assess them. Social-emotional problems make it difficult for learning-disabled students to connect with others socially or in the classroom.

Diagnosis

Diagnosing someone with a learning disability can be a long process. It can be difficult to identify that there's a problem in the first place. Each disability has multiple symptoms. Every person can have a different combination of symptoms, as well as multiple learning disabilities. In addition, the levels of severity involved in the disabilities can vary widely from person to person. Even without knowing they have a learning disability, some children may sense there's a problem and try to camouflage it. Initially, it may appear that the child just doesn't want to go to school or do their homework. Any student with or without a learning disability might want to avoid school or homework for a variety of reasons, so this sign of an issue can be easily misinterpreted.

Some learning disabilities can be diagnosed in early childhood, particularly if there are developmental delays. But most are observed once a child starts school. Once an educator or parent notices a delay or other issue that needs attention, there are a variety of ways to handle the diagnostic process.

Response to Intervention

In some schools, the first step is Response to Intervention (RTI). RTI is used in the classroom for a variety of reasons. It helps teachers identify students who struggle academically in certain subjects. It also

Someone may undergo many tests and evaluations to be diagnosed with a learning disability. In some cases, children may try to hide their disabilities.

helps identify students who have specific academic challenges that are not learning disabilities, such as students who speak English as a second language. RTI is a set of tools to help teachers understand which children are struggling and start to identify why they're struggling. "The goal is for the school to intervene, or step in, and start helping before anyone falls really far behind," says parent advocate and former teacher Amanda Morin.[23]

RTI is not a firm diagnostic tool but rather a way of determining which students are struggling and understanding what the source of the struggle could be. Teachers use RTIs to evaluate students, and then they try different techniques to help those who need it. That can include smaller subsets of students at similar ability levels and learning styles working with different kinds of instruction. It's a tiered approach. At first, the entire class is one full tier. But as assessments are done, students with similar abilities are grouped into smaller tiers to work together. Depending on the needs of the individual students, there may be only two or three tiers. But sometimes the process moves into intensive interventions, which can involve identifying a tier with just one or two students. "RTI isn't a specific program or teaching method," says Morin. "It's a systematic way of measuring progress and providing more support to kids who need it."[24] RTI is a process, with evaluations repeated over time to see how the students are progressing. If they're not progressing, the teacher can regroup and consider different approaches and instructional techniques to help them.

Learning Disabilities Evaluation

First, a teacher identifies someone through RTI or classroom observation who may need additional assistance through an RTI or classroom observation. Once the student is identified, a full individual evaluation needs to be done before the student is eligible for special services. This evaluation is usually done by the school district, but there are also private external sources that can conduct evaluations. Those external sources include local universities, teaching hospitals, community parent resource centers, and the LDAA.

These specific learning disability evaluations are complex, thorough assessments. To qualify for help under the Individuals with Disabilities Education Act, the evaluation must address four standards. The first standard is that the student is performing well below his potential in one or more school subjects. It may also be that the student has been shown to be at risk through the RTI. Second, the learning disabilities identified are severe enough to

The Emotional Side of Learning Disabilities

When someone asked first-grader Natalie Tamburello what she wanted to be someday, she answered, "Smart like everyone else." From an early age, she struggled with dyslexia and some sensory integration issues. By the time she was in middle school, she often ended her school days by getting into her mother's car and bursting into tears.

But what made a difference for Natalie was how her mother responded to her cries of frustration. "In moments like those, my mom wouldn't try to soothe me or tell me to 'just try harder.' She just carved out time for us to talk. She dropped the idea of getting me home to get started on the hours of homework I surely had. Instead, she took me to a quiet place where we could chat."

During those chats, Natalie's mother let her vent and didn't try to interfere with her feelings. Once Natalie was calmer, she and her mother would come up with a plan of action for tackling that day's schoolwork. That helped Natalie feel more in control and more able to face the hard work of homework. "Since I never felt pressured to get perfect grades, I developed my desire to learn on my own terms," she says.

Natalie Tamburello, "How Mom Helped Me Redefine Success When My Dyslexia Got Me Down," *The Inside Track* (blog), *Understood.org*, March 7, 2016. www.understood.org.

require assistance. Then it must be shown that the student has had adequate, appropriate learning opportunities. Finally, other causes for underachievement, such as health or emotional issues, need to be ruled out.

"Clearly, no one test—and no one individual—can possibly be expected to provide all this information," authors Smith and Strick say. "The law therefore requires public school districts to use multidisciplinary teams of professionals in the identification process."[25] The makeup of those multidisciplinary teams varies across school districts. Typically it involves learning specialists, psychologists, speech-language pathologists, occupational and physical therapists, neuropsychologists, and social workers within the school district.

A full evaluation can last several weeks. There are many steps involved. Exactly what the steps are depends on the school district and the student's situation. Among the possible steps is a review of school records and the student's classroom work to assess academic challenges. This may be done along with a review of the school's curriculum and educational materials. The teaching methods used to deliver the curriculum may be assessed as well. The student's medical and social history is likely to be reviewed to rule out any medical cause for the academic problems. There could be time spent observing the student in the classroom and, if needed, at home. Evaluators may conduct interviews with the student and the student's parents or guardians, teachers, and other significant adults. Tests and assessments may be conducted to determine what the student's learning potential is and how he processes information.

Each student is different and faces different challenges. That's why it's important that this evaluation is given all the time and resources necessary to avoid an incorrect diagnosis. Learning disabilities are complex, with a wide-ranging array of symptoms and levels of severity. But people with learning disabilities often have very high potential waiting to be unlocked. Identifying the disability and developing a plan to work with it can help someone achieve their full potential.

Chapter 3

HOW DO LEARNING DISABILITIES IMPACT DAILY LIFE?

People with learning disabilities have a wide range of experiences in terms of how their conditions affect daily life. One twelve-year-old told a teacher, "It's like my mind is a television set, but someone else is working the remote control. Sometimes my life just gets all scribbly."[26] From the time a person wakes up in the morning until she goes to bed at night, her learning disabilities have an impact on her life. It takes an additional emotional toll if family, friends, and teachers don't seem to understand how hard it

Learning disabilities may strain family relationships as family members struggle to understand the experience of a loved one who has a learning disability. The person with a learning disability may feel isolated.

can be. It can even lead to people being incorrectly labeled as lacking intelligence. Being dyslexic or having NLD does not mean someone is not intelligent. It means that her brain processes information differently than someone without a learning disability. That difference affects a person's approach to the tasks of everyday life.

While each disability can have different effects on a person's life, one common outcome is reduced self-esteem. This can happen when people with the learning disabilities see how they struggle in ways others around them don't. It makes it harder for them if parents don't take the disability seriously or understand how it works. It's also hard if teachers think they're lazy or uncooperative. That can prevent the teacher from working with the student to find techniques to bypass the disability. Peers might tease or ignore the student. Anna Koppelman initially didn't care about her dyslexia until her elementary school friends stopped playing with her. "They could read and I could not—which meant they were smart and I was not. The roof of the school was covered in fake grass, and we had tricycles that we could ride during lunch and recess. I remember watching them peddling away into the distance, with their Harry Potter books packed away in their knapsacks and thinking for the first time that I truly was stupid."[27] People who don't understand learning disabilities can have a big emotional effect on those who have them.

> "They could read and I could not—which meant they were smart and I was not. The roof of the school was covered in fake grass, and we had tricycles that we could ride during lunch and recess. I remember watching them peddling away into the distance, with their Harry Potter books packed away in their knapsacks and thinking for the first time that I truly was stupid."[27]
>
> – Anna Koppelman, who has dyslexia

Auditory Processing Disorder

For people without APD, listening to others speak is generally not hard. They can routinely and quickly recognize words and the sounds within the words that differentiate them. That's not the case for someone with APD. Instead, noises and sounds blur together. For that person, the day could start with an irritated parent who thinks he's deliberately not listening. At school, other students may make jokes that he doesn't understand. He has trouble understanding because he can't properly process all the sounds. It's also difficult because subtext and metaphors don't come easily.

While things like music can be enjoyable, they're a distraction if they are part of the background. That background sound can make it even harder to understand what others are saying. The more rapidly someone speaks, the more the person with APD struggles to understand. Speaking louder won't help. Volume isn't the issue—speed is. The mother of a girl with APD says, "There was one third-grade teacher—if Jenny didn't respond to directions right away, this woman got right in her face and started yelling. When she's bombarded with a lot of noise, she shuts down—like a soldier with shell shock."[28]

APD can also impact someone's ability to form and maintain friendships, in which communication is critical. She can have a hard time understanding, much less telling, jokes. Managing a conversation with another person or multiple people can be so hard that she would rather avoid it altogether.

Language Processing Disorder

LPD is one condition that parents are more likely to notice before a child starts school. Children with LPD are slower to speak and use shorter sentences and words. They may not easily understand what others say to them. The problem increases as language becomes more complicated. "A child who can handle 'Bring me the cake mix' with no difficulty may be completely at sea when asked, 'Please unpack the grocery bag, and bring me the cake mix after you put the milk in the refrigerator,'" write Corinne Smith and Lisa Strick in *Learning Disabilities: A to Z.*[29]

Socially, people with LPD may struggle to form friendships and other relationships because communication is so critical in those relationships. If others aren't willing to work with them, they may prefer to be alone, even when they'd like to have friends. But they need friends who can work with them. LPD can also make them easy targets for bullies.

Dyscalculia

People who struggle with numbers and math symbols will be challenged in math classes. But they are also challenged in science classes, which can force them to use mathematical concepts. Dyscalculia can cause issues with sorting and sequencing too. As one mother notes about her daughter, "Our daughter recently confessed that, when she was young, she counted 3, 2, 1, 4 instead of 1, 2, 3, 4. It took years for her to get number sequencing down."[30] Even classes like physical education can be challenging, with many sports requiring players to count and keep track of points.

Dyscalculia also has an impact on life outside of school. Numbers and math are involved in many aspects of everyday life. Numbers are used in cooking, remembering what time to catch the bus, handling money,

> "Our daughter recently confessed that, when she was young, she counted 3, 2, 1, 4 instead of 1, 2, 3, 4. It took years for her to get number sequencing down."[30]
>
> – Mother of a girl with dyscalculia

reading bank accounts, and feeding pets. Dyscalculia can affect using a measuring cup or reading and understanding a map. It can also make things like keeping track of the day of the week or month hard. That can lead to confusion over when school assignments and out-of-school appointments are. Telling time is often an issue as well.

Dysgraphia

Students with dysgraphia may have little to no difficulty reading. But when they try to translate words onto a page by writing, they often find that they struggle. This can start very early. As writer Erica Patino says, "For many children with dysgraphia, just holding a pencil and organizing letters on a line is difficult. Their handwriting tends to be messy. Many struggle with spelling and putting thoughts on paper. These and other writing tasks—like putting ideas into language that is organized, stored and then retrieved from memory—may all add to struggles with written expression."[31] The many steps in between coming up with an idea and putting it on paper can be hard to manage. Sentences and paragraphs may not be complete and can be missing words. Students may struggle with coordinating brain and hand activities,

> "For many children with dysgraphia, just holding a pencil and organizing letters on a line is difficult. Their handwriting tends to be messy. Many struggle with spelling and putting thoughts on paper. These and other writing tasks—like putting ideas into language that is organized, stored and then retrieved from memory—may all add to struggles with written expression."[31]
>
> – Erica Patino, writer

like taking notes while listening to a lecture. They may grip writing tools so hard they cramp their hands. This makes any schoolwork involving handwriting, whether notetaking in class or writing test answers, difficult and time consuming.

But dysgraphia can also be challenging to manage outside of school. Even though many written functions have gone digital, there are still many places where people need handwriting. Many government forms require handwritten signatures. People may have to fill out a handwritten form at the bank or at the Department of Motor Vehicles. Students with dysgraphia are also more likely to struggle with expressing specific ideas or concepts or grasping humor and subtext. That makes it harder for them to communicate with people their age. There are also some people with dysgraphia who struggle with fine motor skills. Things like tying shoes or buttoning clothes can be difficult.

Dyslexia

Words on the page appear different for students who have dyslexia, compared to those without dyslexia. That can cause people with dyslexia to have trouble recognizing letters or have issues processing the letters and the sounds that go with them. Their brains may incorrectly decode the order of letters in a word or substitute similarly sized words. It makes reading assignments—or reading for fun— much more difficult and frustrating. It can often take someone with dyslexia much longer to read the same amount of text as someone without dyslexia. People who have trouble interpreting written words, or putting words on paper, face those challenges in nearly every class

Someone with dyslexia may have trouble traveling. Dyslexia affects navigation skills.

they take. The brain's way of processing written information can also make math difficult.

Dyslexia also affects people outside of school. Reading comprehension is a major part of daily life. People have to read labels on prescription medications, steps in a recipe, street signs, and paperwork for job applications. But dyslexia does not only affect reading. A person with dyslexia may have trouble interpreting social cues and responding appropriately to them. It can be hard for them to make friends and feel that they fit in socially. Even telling left from right can be a challenge. Time management and impulse control are difficult, making it harder for them to make a plan and stick to it.

Navigation skills are another aspect that can be affected as well, making it harder to get from place to place. Koppelman, who has dyslexia, says, "I spent half an hour on 14th Street last week trying to figure out which avenue is Eighth and which is Seventh, and then another half trying to figure out what it meant when the nice woman walking her dog instructed me to turn left."[32] The well-meant advice didn't help her because she had trouble with the basic concepts.

Nonverbal Learning Disability

People with NLD have trouble with social cues. The condition can strain personal relationships, both with family and with potential friends. Humans rely on nonverbal cues—tone of voice, facial expressions—to understand dialogue. For example, someone might say, "Great! That'll be fun," when told to take out the trash. However, the person's body language and tone of voice show that he is feeling the exact opposite.

When the ability to interpret those cues is compromised, it leaves the learner struggling to understand conversations. Someone with NLD can find the social world a bewildering place. She may not be able to recognize the emotional state of others. It can be difficult for her to understand humor or statements that require additional context or subtext. She also may not understand that others expect her not to interrupt when they are talking.

People with NLD are likely to have a hard time managing things like routes and following multistep instructions. Even getting themselves from one spot to another without getting lost and being

People with nonverbal learning disabilities may experience sensory sensitivities to the point where some sensations become nearly intolerable. For example, lights may seem much too bright.

late can be a challenge. These difficulties are in contrast to their stronger verbal skills. Those verbal skills allow them to develop large vocabularies, and they usually have strong memories. They often use those verbal skills to mask the difficulties they're facing. In fact, they may be overly talkative at times, inclined to verbally label information so they can understand it. Unspoken information can be difficult for them to understand. They also tend to ask many questions.

Organization and planning can be challenging for many people, but those things are especially challenging for people with NLD. One student with NLD says, "When I was about seven or eight, my mom would come in and tell me, 'You have to clean your room now.' And I would say, 'okay.' But then I would look at the mess and just throw myself down on the bed and cry. All I knew is that the mess was too big, and I could never do it."[33] Eventually, the student and parent worked out a system that broke the process down into smaller steps, such as making the bed and picking up toys. Approaching a project of any size that has multiple steps can be overwhelming for someone with NLD. She is capable of performing all the steps, but determining what the steps are and in which order to do them is a challenge.

Someone with a learning disability, especially NLD, can experience sensory sensitivities. These sensitivities can cause certain feelings or sensations to become nearly intolerable. This includes anything from noticing a shirt label to feeling as if lights are too bright to tasting certain flavors. One student with NLD explains, "When I first went away from home [to a summer program], I didn't brush my teeth for the entire summer. I know, I know, now it sounds gross, but at the time, I just could not stand the taste of the tap water in the bathroom. And I didn't know what else to do. Now that I'm older, I would know enough to bring some bottled water into the bathroom with me, but at the time that just would not have occurred to me."[34]

Organization and planning can be an issue too. Tera is a student with NLD. Her mother reports, "Tera always did her homework, but she frequently forgot where she put it. She often handed work in late, especially in early grade school. . . . When she copied things out of her book she'd forget the bottom half of the page and end up not doing half of the assignment."[35]

Problems with motor skills are another factor for people with NLD. This can involve gross motor skills, which are things like walking, running, or kicking. It can also involve fine motor skills, which are things like tying shoes, buttoning buttons, writing, or using scissors.

Even balance, like in riding a bike, can be challenging. People with NLD also struggle with changes to routines. As the Nonverbal Learning Disorder Association explains, "Many people with NLD lack the ability to 'wing it' when the unexpected occurs. They may be afraid of new unknown situations and experiences. More than most people, they need to know what will happen next. They really don't like surprises."[36]

Visual Perceptual/ Visual Motor Deficit

People with visual perceptual/ visual motor deficit process visual information differently than others. This means that school tasks such as writing or using scissors to cut things are more difficult. People with the condition can also have poor hand-eye coordination, making it hard to copy something, such as information on a whiteboard. Their handwriting appears messy, and they often hold pencils too tightly, cramping their hands.

This difficulty processing visual information can also affect life outside of school. It can make it harder to do things like memorize phone numbers or sort socks or other items. People with visual perceptual/visual motor deficit also often appear clumsy, easily bumping into things.

"Many people with NLD lack the ability to 'wing it' when the unexpected occurs. They may be afraid of new unknown situations and experiences. More than most people, they need to know what will happen next. They really don't like surprises."[36]

– Nonverbal Learning Disorder Association

They can also exhibit difficulties with time and planning. "These children are notorious for their inability to estimate time accurately," Smith and Strick write. "They are chronically late, and their parents complain that they are never ready to go anywhere, even when they have been given frequent warnings."[37] But their issues with time and planning aren't rooted in wanting to rebel against their parents or teachers. Their brains do not process the information needed to make these plans and account for timing.

Struggling with Self-Perception

Learning disabilities can damage someone's self-confidence and self-esteem. People are not at fault for their learning disabilities. But classmates might distance themselves from someone they think is different. Teachers might assume students are being lazy or misbehaving. Parents might express disappointment in their child's achievements. These things make children feel bad about themselves. "All too often children blame themselves for the problems associated with these handicaps. They assume they are stupid because they do not do well in school, and are unlikable because they do not have hordes of friends. It can be heartbreaking to hear how mercilessly these kids regard themselves," explains Corinne Smith, who has heard many examples of these situations. "One mother remembers her first-grader concluding, 'Mommy, even the dumb kids in the class can do this stuff, so I must be dumber than dumb, whatever that is.'"[38]

If students don't receive the help they need, they can suffer from learned helplessness. A person who expects to fail will find reasons not to try. This pattern can become a vicious cycle. "Once a student stops trying, of course, continued failure is pretty much guaranteed,"

Life as an Adult with Learning Disabilities

Learning disabilities are not something people grow out of. Because there are no cures, people continue working with their disabilities into adulthood. But that doesn't mean they won't be successful. For example, Dan Spencer was diagnosed with dysgraphia and visual processing disorder when he was in second grade. School was a struggle for him. But as he came to understand that having learning disabilities did not mean he was stupid, he found ways to work with his disabilities. He always had trouble with biology class, but he loved spending time outdoors. He figured out a system of different learning styles to help him overcome his struggles. As he continued to find success, he began to consider a career in conservation that would require a college degree—something that hadn't seemed possible when he was young. Today he works as an educator for the US Fish and Wildlife Service, a dream career for him. "While I am a success story, I did have to play a lot of academic catch-up in college despite all the school and parental support I received in my K-12 years," he says. "Others are not as fortunate, so the sooner they acquire a more positive view of their disability and become aware of their intelligences, the better."

Dan Spencer, "Outsmarting My Disability: From Struggling Student to Conservation Educator," *USFWS Pacific Region* (blog), n.d. usfwspacific.tumblr.com.

says Smith.[39] On the other hand, success in one area can encourage someone to try elsewhere.

Regardless of the type of learning disability someone has, there are different strategies and tactics that can help them work with it—or around it. It's important that people reach out for help with developing these strategies and tactics so their self-perception isn't damaged. It's also important for people to recognize that learning disabilities are not caused by lack of intelligence.

Chapter 4

HOW ARE LEARNING DISABILITIES MANAGED?

There are currently no cures or medications for learning disabilities. However, there are many different tools and techniques to help people manage various aspects of their learning disabilities. The techniques that students learn to help with school can be used throughout their lives. With no cure, learning to live with and work around learning disabilities involves skills that are lifelong necessities. The LDAA says, "The impact of learning disabilities is lifelong. The issues that made school work so challenging as a child crop up again in the workplace, in social situations, and in our homes."[40] For example, while people won't have math homework after graduation, they will still have to add up purchases, pay bills, and manage other processes involving math.

Tools exist to help people with these tasks. People who struggle with handwriting can use simple pencil grips. Computers, smartphones, and calculators help people with reading, writing, and number issues. Some technology can read text out loud. High-tech solutions also include software that predicts words for people who have trouble spelling. There are speech recognition programs that can take spoken words and translate them into written text.

> "The impact of learning disabilities is lifelong. The issues that made school work so challenging as a child crop up again in the workplace, in social situations, and in our homes."[40]
>
> –Learning Disabilities Association of America

There are also techniques that have been developed over the years that don't involve technology, but can provide assistance and relief. IEPs allow students to pursue alternative forms of education and teaching for the subjects that are hardest for them. Some alternatives available with an IEP could include special resource rooms staffed by education specialists who bring together smaller groups of students with similar needs. Another educational alternative is an integrated co-teaching classroom, which takes place in the regular classroom but has a special education teacher in place to work with learning-disabled students. An IEP may also give students access to a tutor who can work with them on strategies to work with their disabilities. Although not part of an IEP, there are private schools that specialize in teaching students with different kinds of learning disabilities. There are some techniques that can work for multiple learning disabilities, while others are geared for a particular disability.

Accommodations and Modifications

All forms of learning disabilities can be dealt with using accommodations and modifications. In most public schools, an IEP is required to get these accommodations and modifications. When schools and educators make accommodations for students with learning disabilities, they don't change what the student will learn. They change how the student will learn. This can involve things like allowing a student with reading difficulties to use an audiobook. Even something simple like trying different pens or pencils can make a difference for someone who struggles to write. Allowing students to record class lectures rather than take handwritten notes can be useful. For complex assignments, creating a plan that outlines each step can help the student focus.

There are four categories of accommodations: presentation, response, setting, and scheduling. Presentation changes how the information is given to the student. A student might listen to an audiobook instead of reading the text. Or students may have test questions read out loud to them so they don't have to read the questions themselves. Changing the response focuses on how students complete assignments. A typed assignment could replace a handwritten paragraph. Setting changes may involve providing a separate, quieter room for testing. Scheduling changes can give students more time to complete assignments or tests. The goal of accommodations is to provide students with the resources they need to succeed. "Teachers tend to underestimate these kids," says one parent of a learning-disabled student. "Accepting accommodations should not be accompanied by unnecessary lowering of expectations."[41]

While accommodations focus on how a student learns, modifications might change what is being learned. For example, many schools require third-graders to learn multiplication. But a student with learning disabilities might still be struggling with addition and subtraction. A modification would allow the student to keep working on addition and subtraction without getting a lower grade in math class.

The general principles of accommodations and modifications are the same for all learning disabilities. However, different techniques are used to help students with different disabilities. Because some people have more than one learning disability, techniques are sometimes used together. Multiple tools can be used together to help students succeed at home, in the classroom, and beyond.

> "Teachers tend to underestimate these kids. Accepting accommodations should not be accompanied by unnecessary lowering of expectations."[41]
>
> *–Parent of student with learning disabilities*

Quiet

Quiet is important so students can focus. This can be accomplished in multiple ways. For example, having the student sit in the front of the classroom keeps them away from distractions that can make it harder for them to focus. Another approach is to place students in classrooms with closed doors and windows, which minimizes the amount of noise and distraction in the classroom itself. Students may also be allowed to take tests in separate spaces that are quieter than the general classroom. These approaches are used for students with auditory processing disorder.

One-on-One or Small-Group Instruction

Reading one-on-one with a teacher, aide, or adult volunteer can help a student improve his language processing skills. Another tactic is to have small groups within a classroom, with each group sorted by similar reading levels. The students can then take turns reading to each other. This approach is often used for students with APD or LPD.

Multisensory Approaches

Because people with learning disabilities often learn more efficiently when multiple senses are engaged, some teachers work with multisensory teaching methods. These methods include things like having students use their fingers to spell words in sand or tapping out sounds. One example of multisensory learning is a science lab. In a lab, students are working with their hands, whether it's measuring out ingredients for a chemical concoction or dissecting a frog.

Another example is the use of interlocking cubes to teach math concepts. This is valuable to any student with reading or number-based disabilities, including dyslexia and dyscalculia, as well as APD. "Kids with dyscalculia may benefit from multisensory instruction in math," says Understood, an organization specializing in learning disabilities. "This approach uses all of a child's senses to help her learn skills and understand concepts. It also helps to teach math concepts systematically, where one skill builds on the next. This can help kids with dyscalculia make stronger connections to what they're learning."[42]

Different Materials

Lower-tech solutions include using graph paper to help keep numbers lined up. A blank piece of paper can cover up everything but the math problem being worked on to limit distractions and help the student focus on just that problem. Students can use colored pencils to tell different math problems apart. Students who have difficulty writing can use larger pencils and pens, which may be easier for them to use.

Another solution can be providing plenty of room to write, whether at home or at school. That may mean using wider-spaced paper, unlined paper, or larger sheets of paper. "Students with dysgraphia struggle with planning their words and letters within the space provided," says a parent of a child with dysgraphia. "They also often write large and need extra space to provide their answers. Eliminate some of the frustration by ensuring there is enough space on worksheets (this includes math)."[43]

Alternative reading materials, such as large-print books or audiobooks, are helpful to many students. There are also specialty pens and pencils that can help these students write more comfortably without cramping their fingers. There are special pencil grips that accomplish the same thing. These are helpful for students with dyslexia, dyscalculia, and dysgraphia.

Students are sometimes allowed to use recorders or borrow notes from another student. They may be allowed to answer test questions aloud rather than writing them. Students can also use materials like paper with raised lines. These special papers make it easier to keep letters on the lines. These are useful for several types of learning disabilities, including dyslexia, dyscalculia, and dysgraphia.

Additional Time

Extra time for reading and working on tests is also helpful for many types of learning-disabled students. "Indeed, the most critical accommodation for a dyslexic reader is simply allowing extra time to take a test or complete an assignment," explains Yale University's Center for Dyslexia and Creativity.[44] Like those with other learning disabilities, people with NLD benefit from being given additional time to process information and work on tasks. "Because people with NLD have trouble 'winging it,' it's best not to place them in situations in which speed and adaptability are required," says reporter Ellen Chase. "The world should be made as predictable as possible, with a clear set of rules and expectations."[45]

Assistive Technology

Technology has made a major difference in the lives of many people with learning disabilities. More and more manufacturers of home computers and smartphones are building in forms of assistive technology as standard features.

Wireless amplification systems help the student block out background noise but still hear the teacher. This can help students with auditory processing disorder. Assistive technology for language

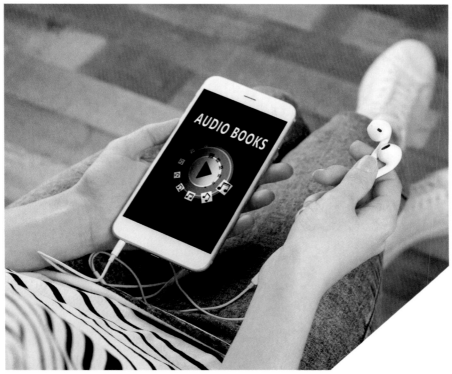

Technology allows many accommodations for students with learning disabilities. For example, audiobooks can help students who may struggle with reading.

processing disorder includes graphic organizers that can help with notetaking. Students can also use voice recorders to record lectures and discussions. For students with dysgraphia, using keyboards and other devices to type projects can make a big difference.

For students with dyscalculia, math notation tools can be used to write or type math symbols and equations. Graphing tools and graphic organizers can help students break down math concepts into smaller pieces. There are a wide range of online and computer programs and apps that act as assistive technology at homework time. Programs like MathTalk have electronic math sheets that allow students to organize, align, and work through math problems on their computers. Things like virtual flashcards and math simulators can help students who struggle with numbers. These programs can be installed on home computers, tablets, and smartphones.

Assistive technology options for students with dyslexia include text-to-speech programs. These are tools that read digital text out loud. There are also pens that read written texts aloud. The reader uses the pen to scan a word or sentence. The pen will then read the scanned words out loud. The pen works without being attached to a computer. There are also highlighting and annotation tools. Display controls help readers set their preferred fonts, font sizes, and colors. Screen masking can close off part of a screen to help the reader focus in on one area.

For students with visual perceptual/visual motor deficit, assistive technology includes using computers for writing projects. It also includes using audiobooks and large-print books for reading. Items like text-to-speech programs and pens that read aloud can also help.

Therapy

Students with language processing disorder may work with a speech therapist or an audiologist. These specialists are trained to work with people who have trouble processing spoken language and have treatment plans and procedures to help them. Speech therapists are specialists with advanced degrees and licenses. They can work with students one-on-one or within the general classroom. There are a variety of strategies they use, including playing and talking to stimulate language development, physically showing students how to produce specific sounds, language drills, and even exercises to strengthen the

The Pros and Cons of Modifications

Modifications are somewhat controversial among educators and parents. Changing what a student learns has both pros and cons. Both the pros and cons should be considered before incorporating a modification into an IEP. "It's true that modifications can make school less of a struggle for students, including kids with learning and attention issues," says Understood. "But the result of modifications can be that a child learns less than his peers. He might fall behind on important skills. Over time, this can put a child at a big disadvantage."

School will be less of a struggle. Some modifications are part of a life-long approach to working with the disability. These modifications include using spell-check rather than memorizing spelling words or listening to audiobooks rather than reading a book.

However, if significant levels of modifications are implemented, it may be hard for the student to earn a high school diploma. Some states require a high school exit exam. Modifications might mean the student hasn't learned what she needs to know to pass the test. Being unable to earn a diploma or pass the high school exit exam makes entering higher education more difficult.

Before committing to an IEP with modifications, a student and her family should understand what specific modifications have been recommended and what the long-term outcome is for them. Some experts recommend working through accommodations first to see if those are sufficient to help the student.

Quoted in Andrew M.I. Lee, "Modifications: What You Need to Know," *Understood.org*, n.d. www.understood.org.

muscles of the mouth. Audiologists are doctors who diagnose and treat hearing and balance problems.

Students with dysgraphia may find working with an occupational therapist helpful too. An occupational therapist works with people to help them develop the skills they need to use on a daily basis. The therapist can work with a dysgraphic student to build muscle strength, dexterity, and hand-eye coordination.

Techniques at Home

One important element of helping students at home is providing a quiet space for schoolwork. This is especially important for students with APD. Studying at the kitchen table while other family members are talking is difficult. Instead, the student should find a quiet space where the door can be closed to help her concentrate.

Regular routines can help a student with LPD at home. This takes away any uncertainty that comes from depending on oral instructions. A parent should give specific directions in a clear tone of voice. "Instead of saying, 'Go get ready, it's time for school,' say, 'Brush your teeth, get your backpack, and put on your coat,'" recommends one special education service.[46]

For students with dyscalculia, home techniques include board games and card games. There are numerous games that give players a workout in basic math concepts. Matching games help people practice matching sets and recognizing patterns. Spatial strategy games, like Connect Four or chess, can help develop spatial recognition. Number strategy games, like the card game Uno, work on thinking strategically about numbers and how to manipulate numbered cards for greatest effect. A game like Monopoly helps people work on counting spaces on the board and managing money.

Students with dysgraphia can do short, quick exercises to relieve tension before beginning homework assignments. These exercises include shaking hands out or rubbing them together. Others use a squeeze ball to strengthen hand muscles. Working with modeling clay can help people strengthen their hand and wrist muscles and improve their coordination.

There are several computer programs that can assist learning-disabled students. These include text-to-speech programs that can read out loud to students.

Students with dyslexia can work on reading skills by listening to audiobooks. These recorded books can help increase reading comprehension. Comic books and graphic novels are valuable too. Having the text in smaller chunks separated by colorful graphics helps the student interpret the words more easily. It's key for a person with dyslexia to find things that truly interest him to read. If he's engaged with the material he's more likely to keep working at it. Short texts from the Internet such as blogs or social media posts offer information in small, easily digestible portions.

NLD students and their families can practice social skills together. Social situations can be frustrating and overwhelming. Practicing situations such as lunchroom conversation at home can help prepare students to cope better at school. Another social technique is meeting people away from school, especially people who aren't inclined to tease and bully. Friendly, out-of-school meetings can help students work on social skills in a safe environment. Some schools offer classes on social skills. These classes are a safe, nonjudgmental environment.

Family members of students with visual perceptual/visual motor deficit should work to make each step of a task clear and separate. Having the student write steps down and number them is helpful. Motor skills can be enhanced by the use of things like puzzles and games. There are many that address hand-eye coordination and can help students with visual perception difficulty.

Relaxation and De-stressing

Relaxation and de-stressing are powerful techniques that apply to every kind of learning disability. Savannah Treviño Casias is a young adult with dyscalculia. She has found success with anti-anxiety techniques including exercise, healthy food, and taking mental breaks. However, she also struggles with negative thoughts. "When I feel anxious, I often have negative thoughts about myself and my abilities. My mind tells me that I'm not good enough or not smart enough or that I'll never be a good student."[47] Instead of focusing on her negative thoughts, Savannah writes down a list of her skills to remind herself that she can do things.

School can be a place where a time-out can be a positive thing. In particular, students with nonverbal learning disabilities can feel overwhelmed with all that's going on in the classroom. Having some time alone can help them calm down and return ready to be involved again.

Having a learning disability does not mean someone cannot succeed in life. There are many famous people who have worked with their learning disabilities and become highly successful. Actor Daniel Radcliffe has dyspraxia, which affects fine motor skills and hand-eye coordination. Director and filmmaker Steven Spielberg, actors Octavia Spencer and Keira Knightley, journalist Anderson Cooper, chef Jamie Oliver, and former NFL quarterback Tim Tebow are all dyslexic. Singer/actor Justin Timberlake, journalist Lisa Ling, and Olympic gold-medal swimmer Michael Phelps have ADHD.

> "When I feel anxious, I often have negative thoughts about myself and my abilities. My mind tells me that I'm not good enough or not smart enough or that I'll never be a good student."[47]
>
> —Savannah Treviño Casias, who has dyscalculia

   Researchers and educators continue to find techniques and approaches that help people with learning disabilities. These advances, combined with a learning-disabled person's willingness work hard, can lead to positive outcomes. Adam Ninyo has dysgraphia, but he has found ways to work around it. He says, "Ultimately, success isn't achieved by grumbling and hitting your head against a wall, desperately trying to do something that you're naturally bad at. It's achieved by acknowledging your disabilities and moving forward to embrace your abilities."[48]

SOURCE NOTES

INTRODUCTION: TWO STORIES OF LEARNING DISABILITIES

1. Savannah Treviño-Casias, "I'm a Successful Student Because I Embrace My Dyscalculia," *The Inside Track* (blog), *Understood.org*, August 4, 2015. www.understood.org.

2. Treviño-Casias, "I'm a Successful Student Because I Embrace My Dyscalculia."

3. Treviño-Casias, "I'm a Successful Student Because I Embrace My Dyscalculia."

4. Treviño-Casias, "I'm a Successful Student Because I Embrace My Dyscalculia."

5. Adam Ninyo, "On Dysgraphia: Writing About the Inability to Write," *Understood.org.* n.d. www.understood.org.

6. Ninyo, "On Dysgraphia: Writing About the Inability to Write."

CHAPTER 1: WHAT IS A LEARNING DISABILITY?

7. "Types of Learning Disabilities," *Learning Disabilities Association of America*, n.d. www.ldaamerica.org.

8. "Types of Learning Disabilities."

9. "What Is a Learning Disability?," *LDOnline,* n.d. www.ldonline.org.

10. Corinne Smith, Ph.D., and Lisa Strick, *Learning Disabilities: A to Z.* New York: Free Press (division of Simon & Schuster), 2010. pp. 6–7.

11. Michael Brian Murphy, *NLD from the Inside Out.* Philadelphia, PA: Jessica Kingsley Publishers, 2016. p. 28.

12. Smith and Strick, *Learning Disabilities: A to Z.* p. 9.

13. Smith and Strick, *Learning Disabilities: A to Z.* p. 10.

14. Smith and Strick, *Learning Disabilities: A to Z.* p. 10.

CHAPTER 2: WHAT CAUSES LEARNING DISABILITIES?

15. Quoted in "Causes of Learning Disabilities." *PBS Parents*. www.pbs.org.

16. Quoted in "Causes of Learning Disabilities."

17. Smith and Strick, *Learning Disabilities: A to Z*. p. 24.

18. Smith and Strick, *Learning Disabilities: A to Z*. pp. 22–23.

19. Murphy, *NLD from the Inside Out*. p. 129.

20. Quoted in Carlin Flora, "How Can a Smart Kid Be So Bad at Math?," *Discover*, December 11, 2013. www.discovermagazine.com.

21. Murphy, *NLD from the Inside Out*. p. 74.

22. Murphy, *NLD from the Inside Out*. p. 83.

23. Amanda Morin, "Understanding Response to Intervention," *Understood.org*, n.d. www.understood.org.

24. Morin, "Understanding Response to Intervention."

25. Smith and Strick, *Learning Disabilities: A to Z*. p. 105.

CHAPTER 3: HOW DO LEARNING DISABILITIES IMPACT DAILY LIFE?

26. Quoted in Richard Lavoie, "What a Learning Disability Really Feels Like," *Scholastic Teacher*. www.scholastic.com.

27. Anna Koppelman, "What I Know Now As a Teen With Dyslexia," *Huffington Post*, December 6, 2017. www.huffingtonpost.com.

28. Smith and Strick, *Learning Disabilities: A to Z*. p. 182.

29. Smith and Strick, *Learning Disabilities: A to Z*. p. 59.

30. Quoted in Lisa Aro, "When Math Just Doesn't Add Up: Understanding Dyscalculia," *ADDitude*. www.additudemag.com.

31. Erica Patino, "Understanding Dysgraphia," *Understood.org*. www.understood.org.

32. Koppelman, "What I Know Now As a Teen With Dyslexia."

33. Murphy, *NLD from the Inside Out*. p. 81.

34. Murphy, *NLD from the Inside Out*. p. 64.

35. Kathy Kirk, "A Mother-Daughter Tale," *NLDline,* n.d. www.nldline.com.

36. "The Paradox of NLD: Nonverbal Learning Disorders in Adults and Children," *NLDline*, n.d., www.nldline.com.

37. Smith and Strick, *Learning Disabilities: A to Z*. p. 56.

38. Smith and Strick, *Learning Disabilities: A to Z*. p. 83.

39. Smith and Strick, *Learning Disabilities: A to Z*. p. pp. 100–101.

CHAPTER 4: HOW ARE LEARNING DISABILITIES MANAGED?

40. "Support and Resources for Adults with LD," *Learning Disabilities Association of America*, n.d. www.ldaamerica.org.

41. Andrew M.I. Lee, "Accommodations: What They Are and How They Work," *Understood.org*, n.d. www.understood.org.

42. "Understanding Dyscalculia," *Understood.org*, n.d. www.understood.org.

43. Amanda Morin, "Multisensory Instruction: What You Need to Know," *Understood.org*, n.d. www.understood.org.

44. "Time and Tools," *Yale Center for Dyslexia and Creativity*, n.d. dyslexia.yale.edu.

45. Ellen Chase, "Children, adults with non-verbal learning disorder develop strategies for using talents, navigating around deficits," *The Star-Ledger*, December 7, 2010, www.nj.com.

46. "Language Processing Disorders (LPD)," *Lutheran Special School & Education Services*, December 2011. www.lsses.org.

47. Savannah Treviño-Casias, "8 Ways I Manage Anxiety From My Dyscalculia," *The Inside Track* (blog), *Understood.org*, May 31, 2016. www.understood.org.

48. Ninyo, "On Dysgraphia: Writing About the Inability to Write."

FOR FURTHER RESEARCH

BOOKS

Shirley Brinkerhoff, *Learning Disabilities*. Broomall, PA: Mason Crest, 2015.

Jennifer Landau, *Teens Talk about Learning Disabilities and Differences*. New York: Rosen Publishing, 2018.

Michael Brian Murphy, *NLD from the Inside Out*. London, Philadelphia: Jessica Kingsley Publishers, 2016.

Robert Reid, Torri Ortiz Lienemann, and Jessica L. Hagaman, *Strategy Instruction for Students with Learning Disabilities*. New York: The Guilford Press, 2013.

Corinne Smith, PhD, and Lisa Strick, *Learning Disabilities: A to Z*. New York: Free Press, 2010.

INTERNET SOURCES

Candace Cortiella and Sheldon H. Horowitz, "The State of Learning Disabilities," *National Center for Learning Disabilities*, 2014. www.ncld.org.

Patricia H. Latham, "Learning Disabilities and the Law: After High School: An Overview for Students," *Learning Disabilities Association of America*, 2018. www.ldaamerica.org

"Tips for Students with Learning Disabilities," *PBS*, n.d. www.pbs.org.

Savannah Treviño-Casias, "I'm a Successful Student Because I Embrace My Dyscalculia," *The Inside Track* (blog), Understood.org, August 4, 2015. www.understood.org.

WEBSITES

Council for Learning Disabilities
www.council-for-learning-disabilities.org

The Council for Learning Disabilities focuses on improving educational experiences for students with learning disabilities.

Learning Disabilities Association of America
www.ldaamerica.org

The LDAA provides supports to people with learning disorders and their families.

National Center for Learning Disabilities
www.ncld.org

This group includes several pages of resources for anyone looking to learn more about learning disabilities.

Smart Kids with Learning Disabilities
www.smartkidswithld.org

This group provides support to parents of kids with learning disabilities.

TeensHealth Learning Disabilities
www.kidshealth.org/en/teens/learning-disabilities.html

This teen-focused site explains common learning disabilities.

IMAGE CREDITS

ABOUT THE AUTHOR

Amy C. Rea grew up in northern Minnesota and now lives in a Minneapolis suburb with her husband, two sons, and dog. She writes frequently about traveling around Minnesota. She's also written about the lost colonists of Roanoke, the lost continent of Atlantis, the Pony Express, the Dust Bowl, and the battle of the Alamo.